W9-CNA-398

THE WAR OF 1812
12 THINGS TO KNOW

by Bonnie Hinman

12 STORY LIBRARY

www.12StoryLibrary.com

12-Story Library is an imprint of Peterson Publishing Company and Press Room Editions.

Produced for 12-Story Library by Red Line Editorial

Photographs ©: Bettmann/Corbis, cover, 1; Virtue, Emmins & Co./Library of Congress, 4; Gianni Dagli Orti/Corbis, 5; Stapleton Collection/Corbis, 6; AS400 DB/Corbis, 7, 9, 18; Public Domain, 8, 12; Library of Congress, 10, 19; Kurz & Allison/Library of Congress, 11, 25, 29; Courtesy of Toronto Public Library, 13, 22; John Rogers/Library of Congress, 14; Leonard de Selva/Corbis, 15; Jacques-Nicolas Bellin, 16; Percy Morgan/Library of Congress, 17, 21, 28; John Bower/Library of Congress, 20; Alexis Chataigner/Library of Congress, 23; E. Percy Moran/Library of Congress, 24; Library and Archives Canada/C-001855, 26; Airman Nick Lyman/US Navy, 27

Content Consultant: Glenn. S. Gordinier, Ph.D., Robert G. Albion Historian Faculty Chair, Williams College-Mystic Seaport Program in Maritime Studies

Library of Congress Cataloging-in-Publication Data
Names: Hinman, Bonnie, author.
Title: The War of 1812 : 12 things to know / by Bonnie Hinman.
Other titles: War of 1812, twelve things to know
Description: Mankato, MN : 12-Story Library, [2017] | Series: America at war
  | Includes bibliographical references and index. | Audience: Grades 4-6.
Identifiers: LCCN 2016002428 (print) | LCCN 2016002589 (ebook) | ISBN
  9781632352699 (library bound : alk. paper) | ISBN 9781632353191 (pbk. :
  alk. paper) | ISBN 9781621434382 (hosted ebook)
Subjects: LCSH: United States--History--War of 1812--Juvenile literature.
Classification: LCC E354 .H56 2016 (print) | LCC E354 (ebook) | DDC
  973.5/2--dc23
LC record available at http://lccn.loc.gov/2016002428

Printed in the United States of America
Mankato, MN
May, 2016

Access free, up-to-date content on this topic plus a full digital version of this book. Scan the QR code on page 31 or use your school's login at 12StoryLibrary.com.

Table of Contents

1 United States Becomes a Major Trade Power

After the American Revolution ended in 1783, the United States quickly became a major player among trading nations. US merchants could sell goods freely to other nations. They could also import goods to sell in the United States. Merchant ships sailed all over the world to buy and sell goods.

During this time, the United States had an uneasy peace with Great Britain. Before the revolution, Great Britain controlled the colonies that would later become the United States. The British hoped the United States would fail as a country. Canada was still a British colony. But many Americans thought Canada would rather be part of the United States.

Great Britain had many problems. It went to war with France on February 1, 1793. The two countries signed a peace treaty in March of 1802. But French leader Napoleon Bonaparte ignored some terms of the treaty. On May 18, 1803,

George Washington led the Continental Army during the American Revolution.

Great Britain again declared war on France.

The United States decided to remain neutral in these wars. This allowed Americans to trade more freely with all other countries. US government leaders reduced the army and the navy. They wanted to save money by having fewer soldiers and ships. But this tactic almost proved disastrous.

14
Number of months Great Britain was not at war with France between 1793 and 1814.

- After the American Revolution, US merchants could trade freely with other parts of the world.
- France declared war on Great Britain in 1793.
- France and Great Britain signed a peace treaty in 1802.
- Great Britain declared war on France again on May 18, 1803.
- The United States reduced its army and navy.

THE LITTLE CORPORAL

Napoleon Bonaparte became the leader of France when he overthrew the French government in November 1799. He was nicknamed "The Little Corporal" because of his short height. Napoleon was a magnificent military leader. He eventually controlled mainland Europe. He created a French health department and introduced the Napoleonic Code of laws.

US Sailors Are Forced into Service

Great Britain had 900 Royal Navy ships on active duty by 1803. The Royal Navy was the pride of Great Britain. But it required more than 130,000 men to work on the ships. Not enough sailors volunteered to fill the jobs. Royal Navy ship commanders filled the gap by impressing, or forcing, men to become sailors. Men who worked for the navy boarded British merchant ships to look for sailors. The men took the sailors by force to join the navy. The sailors seldom resisted. They knew they would be beaten if they did.

By 1805, there was a severe shortage of sailors.

Some British sailors worked on US ships. They found the conditions on US ships were better than the conditions on British ships. Royal Navy ships stopped US vessels to search for British men they could impress into service.

Eventually, Americans were also impressed into service for the Royal Navy. The ship commanders reasoned it was impossible to know for sure if an English-speaking sailor was American or British. Impressed Americans had to prove their nationality. This process took time. In the meantime, the Americans had to work on the British Navy ships.

Ships of the British Squadron

THINK ABOUT IT

Was it possible for British commanders to tell if a sailor was American or British? What ways can you think of to tell which country a person comes from?

US ship owners called for the practice of impressing to end. It often left their ships shorthanded. US government leaders sought a treaty with Great Britain. Great Britain offered a treaty with some trade concessions. It also said it would be more careful not to impress US sailors. But US president Thomas Jefferson refused to submit the treaty to the Senate. He believed it did not offer enough benefits for the United States.

6,000
Number of US sailors impressed between 1807 and 1812.

- Great Britain had 900 active ships by 1803.
- The Royal Navy needed 130,000 sailors to work on the ships.
- Great Britain's shortage of sailors became a crisis by 1805.
- Great Britain began impressing British and US sailors.
- US ship owners called for an end to the practice of impressing.

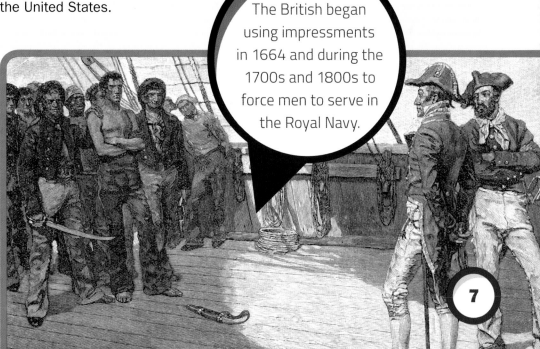

The British began using impressments in 1664 and during the 1700s and 1800s to force men to serve in the Royal Navy.

Free Trade between Nations Is Forbidden

The United States was neutral in the wars between France and Great Britain. So it was free to buy and sell products to all nations. This led to a time of increased prosperity for the new country.

Meanwhile, Great Britain's goal was to defeat France. It did not want anyone to keep it from reaching that goal, including the United States. By 1806, Great Britain decided US shipping was helping the French obtain needed goods for their war effort.

Great Britain passed a series of laws that blockaded some seaports. It also imposed restrictions on trade with neutral nations. France responded with its own restrictions. These new laws forbidding free trade did not sit well with Americans.

Some British sailors working on the blockade ships left to work for the US Navy. They joined the crew of the USS *Chesapeake*. The British wanted to board the *Chesapeake* to search for four deserters. But the *Chesapeake*'s captain and officers refused to let the British board

The *Chesapeake* fired only one shot at the *Leopard*.

their ship. The British ship HMS *Leopard* fired on the *Chesapeake* on June 22, 1807. Three US sailors died.

Six months later, the US government placed an embargo on all US ships departing from US ports. Keeping the ships in port would keep them from being seized by the British or French. It would also protect sailors from being impressed. President Jefferson hoped the embargo would also cause Great Britain and France to relax their policies against neutral nations. US ships carried cargo to and from both countries. If the ships were kept in port, Great Britain and France might suffer from the loss of the goods on those ships.

The embargo did not work. US export values went from $49 million in 1807 to $9 million in 1808. US wealth is based partly on the value of the goods it exports to other countries. Such a drastic drop in one year meant many Americans made a lot less money. As a result, war came creeping closer.

18
Number of sailors wounded on the USS *Chesapeake*.

- The United States was prosperous due to trade with all nations.
- By 1806, the United States was supplying goods to France, and Great Britain put laws in place to prevent it.
- Great Britain and France put laws in place to restrict trade with neutral nations.
- The British fired on the USS *Chesapeake*.
- The United States placed an embargo on all US ships.

President Thomas Jefferson signed the Embargo Act of 1807 into law. It made all exports from the United States illegal.

President Madison Leads the Nation into War

James Madison became president in 1809. He was not sure if the nation should go to war. The Battle of Tippecanoe helped tip the balance.

On November 6, 1811, soldiers marched to Prophet's Town, an American Indian village. Shawnee brothers Tecumseh and Tenskwatawa had founded the village. Tecumseh was a war chief and leader. He worked to join tribes together. He believed that by coming together as a group they could keep settlers from buying or taking American Indian lands.

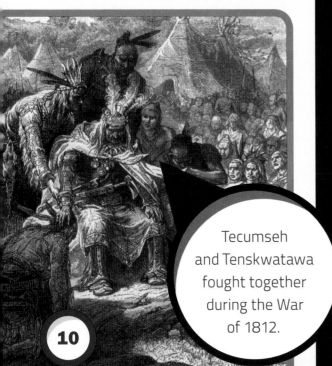

Tecumseh and Tenskwatawa fought together during the War of 1812.

1,000
Number of soldiers Governor Harrison led to Prophet's Town.

- Harrison wanted to force the American Indians to leave the village.
- The American Indians staged an attack, and many people died.
- Many Americans blamed the British because they had given weapons to the American Indians.
- The United States declared war on the British on June 18, 1812.

TECUMSEH AND HIS BROTHER, THE PROPHET

Tecumseh led a confederacy of American Indian tribes. They did not want to give up their land to the United States. His brother, Tenskwatawa, or the Prophet, used religion to unite the tribes. The brothers supported the British during the war. Tecumseh died at the Battle of the Thames in 1813. The Prophet lived for many years after his namesake village, Prophet's Town, was burned.

Indiana Territory Governor William Henry Harrison led the march to Prophet's Town. He was looking for villagers who had led raids on settlements. But the American Indians staged an attack at dawn on November 7. The fight cost many

THINK ABOUT IT

Americans thought Great Britain planned the fight at Tippecanoe. Why do you think they thought this? Do you agree? Why, or why not?

lives on both sides. After the attack, the American Indians fled. Harrison burned the village.

No British soldiers took part in the fight. But the American Indians used British-supplied weapons. Many Americans blamed the British as a result.

By the spring of 1812, President Madison gave up on talking to the British. In early June, he sent a message to Congress asking it to declare war. On June 18, he signed the war declaration. The War of 1812 had begun.

The Battle of Tippecanoe

United States Invades Canada

The United States declared war on Great Britain to keep it from impressing Americans and interfering with US ships. The United States also wanted Great Britain to stop supporting American Indians. The country was currently defending itself. But now it wanted to go on the offensive. This position called for new tactics.

US leaders thought the easiest way to put pressure on Great Britain was to target Canada. It was nearby and sparsely populated. Most Americans thought Canada wanted to be freed from Great Britain. They thought Canadians would want to become part of the United States. They planned to capture Canadian territory.

The United States made several failed attempts to invade Canada in 1812. It soon became clear Canadians did not want to become Americans. The British, Canadians, and American Indians were working together. And they were much better prepared to fight than the Americans.

At the Battle of Frenchtown, Americans wanted to push back the Canadian

Today, a sign marks the spot where US troops crossed the frozen river to attack the British during the Battle of Frenchtown.

3

Number of attempts the United States made to invade Canada in 1812.

- The United States wanted to capture Canadian territory.
- Canadians, the British, and American Indians fought back.
- More than 900 US soldiers were captured or killed at the Battle of Frenchtown.
- Sixty Kentucky prisoners of war were killed by American Indians.
- The United States defeated the British in the Battle of York.

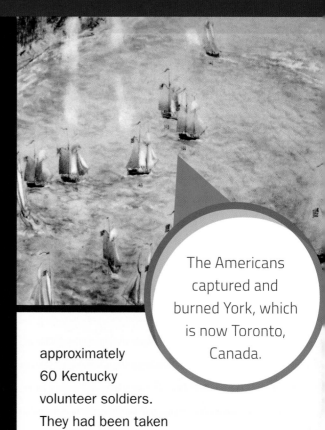

The Americans captured and burned York, which is now Toronto, Canada.

militiamen in the area. This would make Canada easier to invade. The battle took place from January 18 to 23, 1813, in Michigan Territory. It pitted an army of Kentucky volunteers against British troops and their American Indian allies. The Americans won the first fight. But they failed to prepare for the counterattack. The British fought back. They left 900 US soldiers captured or killed. The next day, a group of American Indians killed approximately 60 Kentucky volunteer soldiers. They had been taken prisoner when the US troops surrendered the day before.

On April 27, 1813, US troops defeated the British at the Battle of York on the northern shore of Lake Ontario in Canada. But the British blew up their own powder magazine as they left. The huge explosion killed or injured hundreds of Americans. The remaining US troops were angry because the explosion had killed many of their fellow soldiers. To get even, US soldiers looted and burned the town of York.

War Erupts on the High Seas

Early in the War of 1812, the United States had more success at sea than on land. This was a surprise to both the British and the Americans. The US Navy had only 17 ships.

The US Navy was small, but there was a large fleet of US merchant ships. Some were privateers, or private armed ships. They sailed the seas looking for enemy merchant ships to capture. The cargo of the captured vessels belonged to the privateer ship. Most privateers did not want to fight against enemy warships.

The best-known US naval ship of the war was the USS *Constitution*. It defeated four British ships. It was nicknamed "Old Ironsides" after a shot from the British ship *Guerriere* bounced off the *Constitution*'s hull. But Old Ironsides' hull was made from American live oak rather than iron.

Action between the USS *Constitution* (back) and the *Guerriere* (front)

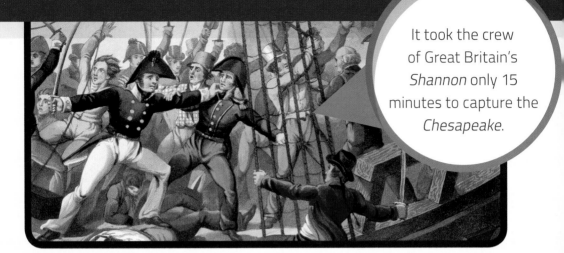

It took the crew of Great Britain's *Shannon* only 15 minutes to capture the *Chesapeake*.

The crew of Great Britain's *Shannon* won an overwhelming victory in a battle against the USS *Chesapeake* on June 1, 1813. The captain of the *Chesapeake*, James Lawrence, suffered a mortal wound in the fight. As he was carried below deck, he called to his men, "Don't give up the ship." In the end, his men had to give up the ship to the British. The British took it as a prize of war. But Lawrence's famous words live on as a motto for the US Navy.

6

Number of well-armed warships the US Navy had in 1812.

- The US Navy had only 17 ships.
- US privateers searched the seas looking for enemy merchant ships.
- The USS *Constitution* defeated four British ships.
- Great Britain defeated the USS *Chesapeake* in June 1813.
- The *Chesapeake* captain said, "Don't give up the ship," which later became the motto of the US Navy.

OLD IRONSIDES

The USS *Constitution* was launched in 1797. Old Ironsides retired from active duty in 1881. But it is still a commissioned ship of war and is the oldest such ship in the world. The wooden ship has been restored many times. It is a symbol of the US naval fleet. Old Ironsides is docked in the Charleston Navy Yard in Boston, Massachusetts.

War Arrives on the Great Lakes

The Great Lakes played a large part in the War of 1812. Soldiers used the lakes to move by ship between Canada and the United States. Great Britain had control of Lake Erie and Lake Ontario before the war began. These lakes were the scene of some major battles.

The Battle of Lake Erie was the most important battle to take place on the Great Lakes. US Master Commandant Oliver H. Perry supervised shipbuilding from his Presque Isle base at the northeast end of Lake Erie. The British Navy patrolled the waters nearby.

Perry's squadron of ships met a British squadron on Lake Erie on September 10, 1813. Perry prepared carefully for the fight. He put sand on the ships' decks. If water splashed on the decks or blood spilled during the fight, the sanded decks would keep the men from slipping.

A 1755 map of New France showing the Great Lakes

4

Number of Great Lakes that share a border with Canada.

- Soldiers used the Great Lakes to move between Canada and the United States.
- Several US ships were built at Presque Isle.
- British and US ships took part in the Battle of Lake Erie on September 10, 1813.
- The United States considered its win a huge victory.
- The British downplayed their loss.

The fighting was fierce, as the ships traded shots from their guns. After two hours of fighting, Perry's ship was disabled. Sailors rowed him to another US ship in the squadron, the *Niagara*. From there, Perry directed the rest of the fight. Within three hours, all six of the British ships surrendered.

Americans celebrated Perry's victory on Lake Erie. The British said the battle was of little importance. But it gave the United States control over Lake Erie and most of the region. The victory on the lake paved the way for the United States to control much of the area. From June to December, the British Navy blockaded the US coast. This choked the US Navy and its merchant fleet.

Perry left his ship, the *Lawrence*, because it was under heavy fire. He was taken to the *Niagara* to continue the fight.

Washington, DC, Goes Up in Flames

For the United States, the lowest point in the War of 1812 came in August 1814. The British targeted the Chesapeake Bay area of Maryland. Months earlier, they had sailed into the bay with 20 warships and several transport ships of troops. They landed at Benedict, Maryland, 60 miles (97 km) from Washington, DC. The capital was not prepared for an enemy attack. It had no defense plan.

On August 24, 1814, the British Army marched toward the capital after defeating US forces at the Battle of Bladensburg. Many Washington residents fled the city before the British arrived.

At the White House, there was a lot of confusion. President Madison was with US troops in the field. His wife, Dolley, packed up documents and other valuables from the White House. When the order came to leave, Dolley swept through the dining room and collected

Dolley Madison ordered the frame to be broken and the canvas removed from the portrait of George Washington. It had been screwed to the wall and was too much work to take down intact.

18

The British burned many important buildings in Washington after their victory in the Battle of Bladensburg.

some silverware. At the last minute, she ordered that a famous painting of George Washington be removed and saved.

When the British arrived at the White house, several officers found the table set for dinner. The evening's meal was still in the kitchen. They sat down and ate a fine feast and drank President Madison's wine. When they finished eating, they torched the building. Meanwhile, other troops burned the Capitol building and all other government buildings, except the Patent Office. They blew up arsenals of weapons and gunpowder.

The British left the capital on August 25. Their next target was Baltimore. It was the third-largest city in the United States. It was near Washington, DC, and was the base for many US privateers. It had much loot for the British to take. The city also was well known for being anti-British.

4,500
Number of British troops that landed at Benedict, Maryland.

- On August 24, 1814, the British Army marched toward Washington, DC.
- The British burned all government buildings, except the Patent Office.
- Dolley Madison saved valuable items from the White House.

British Attack Baltimore

After their success in Washington, DC, the British turned toward Baltimore. It was a prime target. But unlike leaders in the capital, leaders in Baltimore were expecting the British. They had made preparations.

An army of 4,500 men landed at North Point on September 12, 1814. They marched toward Baltimore. The British won a battle about halfway to Baltimore. But they retreated when they saw the mile of trenches and earthworks the people of Baltimore had built, including a large earthen fortress on top of Hampstead Hill.

Meanwhile, the British Navy sailed up the Patapsco River to attack Baltimore by water. To reach the inner harbor, the British passed Fort McHenry. They fired more than 1,500 rounds at the fort over a 24-hour period on September 13 and 14. But damage to the fort was minimal.

At 6:30 a.m. on September 13, 1814, the British began to attack US troops at Fort McHenry.

THE ROCKETS' RED GLARE

The rockets that lit up the sky for Francis Scott Key were Congreve rockets. They looked like skyrockets with a head, a cylinder, and a long stick. They were easy to fire, cheap, and noisy. They made a stir when they whizzed over a battlefield or ship. But they were very inaccurate. Sometimes they returned and hit the soldiers who fired them.

The siege of Fort McHenry was Francis Scott Key's inspiration for writing the poem that became the US national anthem, "The Star-Spangled Banner." Key watched the battle from a British ship. He had gone to the British ship to negotiate the release of a friend who was a British prisoner. In the morning, he saw the US flag still waving over Fort McHenry. The British retreated down the river, ending the bombardment. The Americans had won the Battle of Baltimore.

2
Number of directions the British came from to attack Baltimore.

- British soldiers marched toward Baltimore.
- The soldiers saw the defenses at Baltimore and retreated.
- The British Navy fired more than 1,500 rounds at Fort McHenry.
- Damage to the fort was minimal.
- The siege of Fort McHenry inspired "The Star-Spangled Banner."

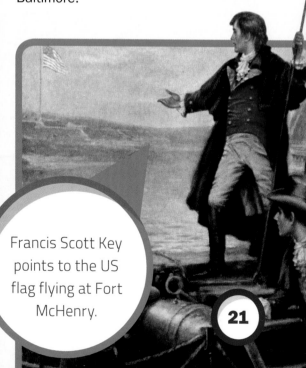

Francis Scott Key points to the US flag flying at Fort McHenry.

Peace Treaty Signed on Christmas Eve

Peace talks between the United States and Great Britain began almost as soon as the war started. Within a week of the declaration of war in June 1812, US leaders sent their peace terms to Great Britain.

Great Britain rejected the terms. British leaders assumed the United States would not go to war. Many of the laws stopping neutral trade were lifted before war was declared. Some historians believe faster communication across the Atlantic Ocean might have stopped the war before it began. Since it took many weeks for ships to sail across the Atlantic, negotiations often stalled.

The final push to peace began in Ghent, Belgium, in August 1814. By then, both sides wanted to end the

With the signing of the Treaty of Ghent, the British recognized the United States as its own nation.

5

Number of weeks it took for a ship to cross the Atlantic.

- Peace talks began at Ghent, Belgium, in August 1814.
- The United States and Great Britain could not agree at first.
- The final treaty was signed on December 24, 1814.

THINK ABOUT IT

The first permanent Atlantic communication cable went into service in 1866. It was placed in the Atlantic Ocean. Messages could then travel quickly between Washington and London. Do you agree with historians that faster communication might have stopped the war? Why, or why not?

war. Napoleon Bonaparte had given up the throne, ending the war in Europe. And the British people were tired of paying high taxes to support the war overseas.

At first, peace talks centered on stopping the British from impressing US sailors and their desire to keep the land they gained during the war. Finally, British and US leaders agreed to terms that gave neither nation a victory.

When the Treaty of Ghent was finished, it did not mention impressments. It returned all land to the nations that had owned it before the war. American Indian tribes, as well as their lands, were to be restored to the status they had held in 1811. Both nations signed the treaty on Christmas Eve in 1814. The War of 1812 was over at last.

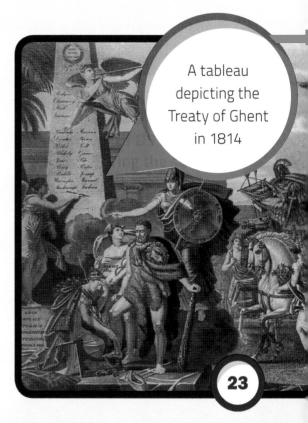

A tableau depicting the Treaty of Ghent in 1814

23

Americans Win Final Battle at New Orleans

It took a long time for news to travel overseas. With no news about the treaty, the British moved to attack New Orleans. A large British force arrived by ship near New Orleans on December 13, 1814. The nation that controlled New Orleans would have control of the Mississippi River.

The easiest way to attack New Orleans was by water. But the British did not have enough boats. There were many ways to attack New Orleans by land. But swamps, cypress groves, and dense undergrowth made the land difficult to cross.

US Major General Andrew Jackson arrived in New Orleans on December 1, 1814. He found the city was not ready to defend itself against an attack. He ordered troops to block waterways and put weapons in place. He also had them build fortifications southeast of New Orleans.

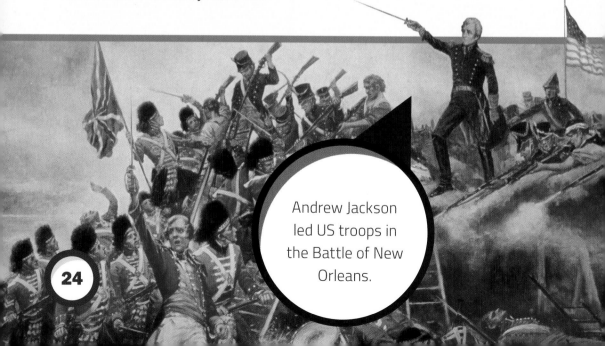

Andrew Jackson led US troops in the Battle of New Orleans.

The British and the Americans met at dawn on January 8, 1815.

The British attacked Jackson's smaller army on January 8, 1815. US forces attacked British troops as they tried to storm the fortifications. Without more ships, the British Navy could not reach New Orleans by water to support the army.

When the smoke of the battle cleared, 2,000 British soldiers were dead, injured, or captured. Jackson's army had just 71 casualties, with only 13 killed. It was the worst defeat in British military history.

39

Number of days Andrew Jackson had to get New Orleans ready for battle.

- The British wanted control of the Mississippi River.
- They attacked New Orleans on January 8, 1815.
- The British Navy lacked boats, and the land was difficult for troops to cross.
- There were 2,000 British casualties and only 71 US casualties.

BARATARIAN PIRATES

A group of men called the Baratarian pirates helped the United States in the Battle of New Orleans. The Baratarians were well known for smuggling and seizing merchant ships. General Jackson called them bandits, but he accepted their help. He needed their weapons. After the war, President Madison forgave the Baratarians of any crimes they had done.

War's End Leaves Important Changes

The US Congress ratified the Treaty of Ghent on February 16, 1815, more than a month after the Battle of New Orleans. After the war, the nation gained confidence as an independent country. Symbols, such as "The Star-Spangled Banner" and the US Navy motto "Don't Give Up the Ship," came out of this war. It was also the start of the US Industrial Revolution.

Canada ended up a winner in the war. Before the war, it was a loosely organized group of colonies. The War of 1812 helped Canadians see themselves as a unified country. Canada became an independent country on July 1, 1867.

The American Indians gained none of the land or concessions promised in the treaty. The United States ignored this provision. Great Britain made no effort to hold the United States to this part of the treaty. More than a million settlers had poured into what had been American Indian territory.

Canada's founding leaders met in 1864 and 1866 to discuss the nation's independence from Great Britain.

Great Britain did not gain land or trade concessions from the war. But it did gain knowledge. The British realized how costly and hard it was to defend Canada's vast borders against invaders. They knew they needed the United States as an ally rather than an enemy. Many years of cooperation between Great Britain and the United States began soon after the War of 1812 ended.

In the War of 1812, the United States proved it could hold its own in the world. Great Britain decided to change its former colonies and enemy into an ally.

54

Number of days it took for the Treaty of Ghent to be ratified by the US Congress.

- After the war, the United States gained confidence as an independent country.
- Canada's separate colonies unified.
- American Indian tribes did not get the land and concessions promised in the treaty.
- Great Britain found out it was easier to be an ally of the United States.

Today, reenactments of battles from the War of 1812 take place in many parts of the United States.

12 Key Dates

June 22, 1807
The British ship HMS *Leopard* fires on the USS *Chesapeake.*

November 7, 1811
The Battle of Tippecanoe takes place in Indiana Territory.

June 18, 1812
President Madison signs a bill declaring war against Great Britain.

January 18–23, 1813
The Battle of Frenchtown takes place and ends in massacre.

April 27, 1813
The United States captures and burns York.

June 1, 1813
Great Britain wins a sea battle against the USS *Chesapeake.*

September 10, 1813
The United States wins the Battle of Lake Erie.

August 24, 1814
The British burn Washington, DC.

September 13–14, 1814
The United States successfully defends Baltimore.

December 24, 1814
The United States and Great Britain sign the Treaty of Ghent in Belgium.

January 8, 1815
The United States wins the Battle of New Orleans.

February 16, 1815
US Congress ratifies the Treaty of Ghent, ending the war.

Glossary

concessions
Things that are granted or given up; often land or privileges.

confederacy
An alliance of people or groups.

counterattack
An attack in response to an enemy attack.

embargo
A government order that keeps ships from moving in or out of a nation's ports.

fortifications
Walls, earth mounds, or forts that protect and strengthen an army's position.

mortal
Causing or likely to cause death; fatal.

neutral
Does not take part in a war between other nations.

powder magazine
A place where ammunition and explosives are stored.

siege
To surround a city and prevent movement in and out; usually includes military attacks.

squadron
A part of a naval fleet of ships.

For More Information

Books

Krull, Kathleen, and Steve Johnson. *Women Who Broke the Rules: Dolley Madison*. New York: Bloomsbury USA, 2015.

Laxer, James, and Richard Rudnicki. *Tecumseh*. Toronto: Groundwood Books, 2012.

Papp, Lisa. *The Town That Fooled the British: A War of 1812 Story* (Tales of Young Americans). Ann Arbor, MI: Sleeping Bear Press, 2011.

Radomski, Kassandra. *Mr. Madison's War: Causes and Effects of the War of 1812* (Cause and Effect). Mankato, MN: Capstone Press, 2013.

Visit 12StoryLibrary.com

Scan the code or use your school's login at **12StoryLibrary.com** for recent updates about this topic and a full digital version of this book. Enjoy free access to:

- Digital ebook
- Breaking news updates
- Live content feeds
- Videos, interactive maps, and graphics
- Additional web resources

Note to educators: Visit 12StoryLibrary.com/register to sign up for free premium website access. Enjoy live content plus a full digital version of every 12-Story Library book you own for every student at your school.

Index

About the Author

Bonnie Hinman has written more
than 35 nonfiction books. She lives
in Joplin, Missouri, with her husband,
Bill, and near her children and five
grandchildren.